to Jesus we sing

© Copyright 2016- Jamie Harvill

All rights reserved. Permission is granted to copy or reprint portions for any noncommercial use, except they may not be posted online without permission.

Wyatt House books may be ordered through booksellers or by contacting:

WYATT HOUSE PUBLISHING
399 Lakeview Dr. W.
Mobile, Alabama 36695
www.wyattpublishing.com
editor@wyattpublishing.com

Because of the dynamic nature of the Internet, any web address or links contained in this book may have changed since publication and may no longer be valid.

Cover and interior design by: Mark Wyatt

ISBN 13: 978-0-9915798-5-3

Printed in the United States of America

Scripture quotations unless otherwise noted are from The New King James Version. Copyright, 1979,1980,1982, Thomas Nelson, Inc., publisher.

to Jesus we sing

A CONCISE HISTORY OF CHRISTIAN WORSHIP

JAMIE HARVILL

author of *Worship Foundry*
and co-writer of "Ancient of Days"

Wyatt House Publishing
Mobile, Alabama

What people are saying about
to  we sing

"This resource is helpful for those looking for a broad understanding of the flow of historical river of worship without being lost in tributaries. The author presents a helpful overview of worship from both a biblical to a Western world view. This resource is an excellent bible study that both informs and reminds the tenets of meaningful worship."

Dr. Michael Eckelkamp
Pastor, St. Johns Church
Denver, Colorado

"A very thoughtful and balanced overview of the history and ongoing unfolding and progression of worship. A comprehensive yet user friendly read and a very useful tool for all aspiring and developing worshippers."

Randy Rothwell
Worship Leader
Integrity Music

"In a time when worship music has become such an important part of our church gatherings, it is more important than ever for church leaders to understand and be able to teach the 'why and how' of worship according to Scripture and church history. Having this solid foundation adds a deeper level of purpose, joy and enthusiasm to our singing when the church gathers. I appreciate the concise chronological teaching from Jamie and the condensed format that is easy to digest and understand. This is a must read for any church leader."

Jimi Williams
VP, Creative
Capitol CMG Publishing / Worship Together

In *To Jesus We Sing*, Jamie Harvill takes what would otherwise be mundane historical facts and trivia and, through his own passion for the Christ, brings to life the worship practices of believers from the Old Testament, through the early church, the Protestant Reformation, the Great Awakenings, right up through the Jesus Movement of the 20th Century. *To Jesus We Sing* is a must read for all worship leaders in today's evangelical church.

Rodney D. Whaley, DMin
Assistant Professor of Worship and Music
Instructional Mentor
Center for Worship/School of Music
Liberty University

Preface

Worship has always been and remains a mystery to me since the first time my grandmother took me to her church as a young child. Enormous and breathtaking stained glass windows—Big Stories, including tales of Jesus and the disciples—filled the otherwise dull sanctuary with delight. The pastor's sermon sounded to me like Charlie Brown's teacher (a guitar through a wah-wah pedal), but the narratives that reflected through those windows conveyed a huge, transcendent Story that seemed to reach out and call me by name. I would one day answer that "call" when, at the age of fourteen, the Holy Spirit pricked my heart with the love of Jesus, and my life would never be the same. I became a part of the Big Story, along with grandma and countless other Christ-followers on the journey of worship. It wasn't until I knew Christ personally that I would connect passion for Christ with the practice of worship. Since then, my desire in life and ministry has been to worship Jesus wholeheartedly and passionately.

The writing of this booklet comes as a result of observing worship leaders, who in their ministries have lacked a basic understanding of Christian worship from an historical perspective. Many are unaware of the reason certain traditions began, and why particular rituals either survived or perished over the centuries. I myself spent many years leading worship with a mottled knowledge of why we do what we do in evangelical worship services.

To help illustrate this, I recall the story of an eager newlywed wife who fixed Sunday dinner for the first time. When the roast was proudly presented on the table, a small amount from both sides of the beef was missing. Gently, the young husband asked his new bride why this was so. She replied, "My mom does it this way." Later that month, while having Sunday dinner at the bride's mother's home, the young man noticed the same oddity with her mom's roast. After bravely inquiring about this, mom-in-law declared, "I don't know, my mother did it this way!" The next week, the bride's grandmother asked the newlyweds over to dinner. In the middle of the table sat a chuck roast with its sides removed. Cautiously, the young man asked the grandma-in-law why her roast was missing its sides—maybe this time he'd get an actual explanation. She responded, "I only have one pan for the oven, and it's small; in order for the roast to fit I need to cut off a bit from both sides." A-ha! Grandma's unusual roast tradition began with a very practical purpose, the significance of which had been lost to the following generations.

Many times, successive generations may lose the meaning and importance of certain customs. This is no different with church history and the Big Story of redemption and worship. Therefore, through extensive scriptural and historical research I have attempted, within a limited space, to visit what I consider to be *key accounts in the metanarrative of worship history*. Please forgive me if, in your opinion, I have left out a significant event or person. *The purpose of this presentation is to offer a very concise history that gives an overview of the practice of worship throughout consecutive generations of the church.*

Again, in this study it was interesting to observe which practices became central in worship over time and which became peripheral or even non-existent. The early church fathers fought boldly against heresy and ungodly influences to defend the Word of God, having left a great impact on worship practices. But it was everyday common people and their passion for Christ that kept worship always evolving and reforming.

It is my desire to make this booklet *very approachable* to Christ-followers in general, but to worship leaders in particular. My friend Mark Wyatt says that most people don't finish the books they start. So, it is my intent for this to be read in a couple of sittings, and for the information gleaned within its pages to be treasured for a lifetime.

You will find questions for each section of history at the end of the booklet, designed for personal use, small groups or for academic purposes. Do not let the brevity of this book fool you; the information enclosed is robust enough to be used for a university class, but is also life giving for the individual as well as for any group. I pray that the time spent in the final section regarding Postmodernism (a little more lengthy than the other sections) will help readers understand the cultural challenges facing young worshipers today, and how churches must be willing to adjust their preferences in order to reach new generations for Christ.

The book title comes from a song I co-wrote with Nancy Gordon called "Because We Believe." Found at the end of each chorus of the modern hymn, the words "to Jesus we sing" express the church's yearning across the ages to worship in song—even as congregational singing was virtually silent for one thousand years.

Thank you for traveling with me through this Big Story of worship. May your hearts be enlightened and encouraged along the way.

Jamie Harvill
Mobile, Alabama

January 2016

Acknowledgments

My journey as a Christ-follower, worship leader, songwriter, author and minister, serving alongside leaders in churches all over the U.S. and the world, has allowed me to observe and study with some of the greatest teachers, theologians, preachers, musicians and composers of our generation. Much gratitude is due to mentors such as Gerrit Gustafson and Marty Nystrom, and influences from my days as a songwriter and worship leader with Integrity Music and Maranatha! Music. I am also indebted to those who have invested in my academic growth, beginning with various professors during my undergraduate years at the University of Mobile (Mobile College), to my professors in graduate school at Liberty University—in particular to Dr. Vernon Whaley, along with his brother, Dr. Rodney Whaley.

My utmost gratitude, aside from my Lord Jesus, belongs to my wife, Brenda, who loves, supports, prays and partners with me in life, family and ministry. Our greatest treasure on earth is our love for and deep devotion to each other, and the fruit of over thirty years together: our wonderful children and grandchildren.

Also, I thank my grandmother, Marie Rye Ethington, for taking me to church in those early days, and for outshining those stained glass windows with her love, worship and devotion to Christ.

Table of Contents

Introduction	*17*
Worship and the Old Covenant: Abraham, Moses and Joshua	*20*
Worship and the Temple: David	*23*
Worship in the Babylonian Exile: The Synagogue	*26*
Worship and the New Covenant: Jesus	*27*
Worship at Pentecost	*30*
Worship In the Early Church	*31*
Worship in the 2ND and 3RD Centuries	*34*
Worship in the 4TH and 5TH Centuries	*37*
Worship during the Medieval Period	*38*

WORSHIP AND THE REFORMATION	*40*
DIVERSE WORSHIP	*43*
WORSHIP AND THE AWAKENINGS IN EUROPE AND AMERICA	*45*
WORSHIP AND THE GREAT REVIVALS OF THE 19TH THROUGH THE 21ST CENTURIES	*47*
POSTMODERNISM AND THE FUTURE OF WORSHIP IN THE CHURCH	*53*
CONCLUSION	*60*
BIBLIOGRAPHY	*65*
STUDY QUESTIONS	*73*

Introduction

"God is not required to establish a relationship with human beings. He is self-sufficient and complete,"[1] says Dr. Vernon Whaley. It would be an egotistical statement to say God "needs" human beings. Even so, "He chose to fellowship with his best creation, man and woman. Deep inside the heart of man, he created a desire for worship."[2] Revelation 4: 11 provides an overview for the purpose of worship: "Worthy are You, our Lord and our God, to receive glory and honor and power; for You created all things, and because of Your will they existed, and were created" (NASB). Through Genesis 1:26 it can be seen that God created man to reflect His own nature.

---

1   Elmer L. Towns and Vernon M. Whaley, *Worship Through the Ages: How the Great Awakenings Shape Evangelical Worship* (Nashville: B&H Academic, 2012), Kindle Edition, location 143.
2   Ibid., location 157.

Gary Mathena says believers are to "...show extravagant devotion to God—to find our joy in Him and Him alone—and to worship God with every fiber of our being."[3] To provide a one-stop definition of worship is impossible, due to its magnitude. Even so, Robert Schaper has provided a strong description: Worship is "the expression of a relationship in which God the Father reveals himself and his love in Christ, and by his Holy Spirit administers grace, to which we respond in faith, gratitude, and obedience."[4] A rather concise characterization comes from Warren Wiersbe, who writes, "Worship is the believer's response of all that he is— mind, emotions, will and body— to all that God is and says and does."[5]

Genuine worship, according to scholar Andrew Hill, is a "quest for God not out of obligation or duty but freely and earnestly in gratitude for his goodness."[6] One's undying devotion is owed to the Creator God. With this understanding, true worship is more relation-

---

[3] Gary M. Mathena, DMin, *One Thing Needful: An Invitation to the Study of Worship* (Nashville: Crossbooks, 2013), 11.

[4] Robert N. Schaper, *In His Presence* (Nashville: Thomas Nelson, 1984), 15-16.

[5] Warren Wiersbe, *Real Worship Real: It Will Transform Your Life* (Nashville: Oliver Nelson Books, 1986), 27.

[6] Andrew E. Hill, *Enter His Courts with Praise: Old Testament Worship for the New Testament Church* (Grand Rapids: Baker Books, 1993), 3.

al than ritual, and those called by God with a believing heart are compelled to draw near to Him for one's very sustenance. Isaiah 55:3 says: "Incline your ear and come to Me. Listen, that you may live; and I will make an everlasting covenant with you, according to the faithful mercies shown to David" (NASB, italics added). 1 Peter 2:9 states the purpose for redemption through Christ, and God's ultimate design for humanity: "But you are a chosen race, a royal priesthood, a holy nation, a people for God's own possession, *so that you may proclaim the excellencies of Him* who has called you out of darkness into His marvelous light" (NASB).

Between creation and the fall, God and man enjoyed an unbroken fellowship, but this friendship would eventually crumble when Adam and Eve, through disobedience, fled from the Garden, leaving the God with whom they once walked, talked, and loved. Sin would separate the first couple from God, from their place of rest, and from worship. As mankind inhabited the planet, God witnessed the great chasm that was deepening between man and Himself through sin. In one instance the people of Babel, in a misguided, self-centered attempt, tried to reach God by building a tower from earth to heaven. God scattered them and confused their language—showing that man cannot reach God or worship

Him by one's own effort (Gen. 11: 1-9). God's ultimate desire was to bridge the gap between Himself and wayward man. He continued to interact with key individuals through the generations, and shaped a metanarrative in the Old Testament of God's divine revelation of Himself.

WORSHIP AND THE OLD COVENANT: ABRAHAM, MOSES AND JOSHUA

Abraham demonstrated what it meant to be a living sacrifice in the offering of his son, Isaac—a reminder that worship is costly. Though an imperfect and flawed human being, he trusted and believed God for the impossible. The difficult decisions he would make in light of God's call set an example of faith, obedience and worship for Christians to follow. In response to God's invitation, Abraham worshiped through obedience. These attributes, among many others, must be nurtured in the hearts of true worshipers today. Through Abraham, several worship practices were developed, including building an altar to the Lord (Gen. 12:17), bowing to the Lord (Gen. 17:17), and paying the tithe (Gen. 14:20).

With Moses the Old Covenant was established. God called a private meeting with him, all the while establishing basic structural elements for a meeting between God and man—informing even modern worshipers that—(1) God initiates it; (2) God establishes a structure of responsibility; (3) God proclaims His Word to the people; (4) God requires personal commitment and renewal; and (5) the covenant must be ratified in blood.[7] The basic covenant was that the Lord agreed to be the God of Israel, and Israel agreed to worship and obey the Lord.[8]

Two great worship lessons come from the story of Moses: to *crave* God's presence—privately and publically with other believers—and to *cultivate friendship* with God.[9] During this time the *Shema*, found in Deuteronomy 6:4–9, functioned as the heart of morning and evening Jewish prayer. It called for a wholehearted love for God and a commitment to share it with their children and families on a daily basis. One modern Jewish commentator said of the Shema: "Engraving this counterintuitive idea into our psyches is our greatest challenge, but key to developing a true appreciation for, and a relationship with, our Creator."[10]

---

7   Robert E. Webber, *Worship Old And New* (Grand Rapids, MI: Zondervan, 1994), 21.

8   Ibid., 22.

9   Vernon M. Whaley, *Called to Worship: The Biblical Foundations of Our Response to God's Call* (Nashville: Thomas Nelson, 2009), 82.

10   Jewish Practice, Chabad.org, "An Overview of the Shema," http://www.chabad.org/library/article_cdo/aid/862695/jewish/An-Overview.htm (accessed August 10, 2015)

Joshua's contribution to the biblical narrative and to worship demonstrates a great devotion to God and a deep desire to obey Him. The preparation given by his mentor Moses was critical for his future ministry. Joshua was a great military commander and, like Moses, an effective leader who knew how to motivate others. After crossing the Jordan, at a place he called Gilgal, Joshua commissioned an altar of twelve stones to be built—each stone representing a tribe of Israel. It stood as a permanent reminder of their sovereign and powerful God. Before the siege at Jericho, Joshua had an encounter with whom many believe to be Christ Himself—The Commander of the Lord's Army (Josh. 5:14). Like Moses, Joshua was told to remove his shoes while standing on holy ground. This is a lesson about respect and honor in worship; one must show reverence in the presence of the Lord.

The Tabernacle was developed under Moses' leadership and used from the time of the Exodus from Egypt through the conquering of the land of Canaan. It was the portable house of the Lord—the place where the Ark of the Covenant and the glory of God dwelt among the people of Israel (Exod. 25-29). The Tabernacle introduced much symbolism, with sacred rituals that expressed the relationship between God and man.[11]

---

[11] Robert E. Webber, *Worship Old & New*, 34.

Priests—whose role it was to minister to God on behalf of the people and minister to the people on behalf of God—were specifically chosen to lead the ceremonies (1Chron. 15:2; Heb. 9).

WORSHIP AND THE TEMPLE: DAVID

David, as flawed as he was, made great and lasting contributions to worship. Though he was unable to build the Temple himself (1 Kings 5:3), he coached his son Solomon for the task. David brought organization to worship and commissioned leaders such as Chenaniah, Heman, Jeduthun and Asaph to systematize, train and lead worshipers in the Temple. Priests led worship, along with every musician and singer, who were all from the Tribe of Levi.[12]

After the building of the Temple in about 900 BC, ritual became lavish and spectacular. Musical instruments accompanied choirs with members numbering in the hundreds. The Roman *Letter of Aristeas* gives an account of some of the activity in the Temple, describing seven hundred ministers there with multitudes

---

12   Elmer L. Towns and Vernon M. Whaley, *Worship Through the Ages,* location 424.

awaiting their sacrifices to be offered. Aristeas observes, "Everything is performed with reverence and in a manner worthy of the Divine Majesty."[13]

Worship in the Temple was well organized and grand; professionals led the music—talented, trained and "ordained" directors, singers, artists and instrumentalists.[14] Not only were music and singing customary in the Temple, but use of banners, dance and feasting were enjoyed as well. Central to worship in the Temple were animal sacrifices. Offerings were given in devotion, and the smell of roasting flesh, along with incense, must have made the worship experience a celebration for the senses.[15]

David was a man of musical talent as he wrote songs, played an instrument and sang. Also a devoted worshiper, David's close relationship with God was cultivated during his life, with his time as a shepherd, and through the period of exile while running from Saul and beyond. Much of David's adventures were reflected in

---

13 Andrew Wilson-Dickson, *The Story of Christian Music: From the Gregorian Chant to Black Gospel—An Illustrated Guide to All the Major Traditions of Music in Worship* (Oxford, England, UK: Lion Books, 1992), 18-19.

14 Donald P. Hustad, *Jubilate II: Church Music in Worship and Renewal* (Carol Stream, IL: Hope Publishing, 1993), 76.

15 Elmer L. Towns and Vernon M. Whaley, *Worship Through the Ages,* location 454.

the Psalms as poems and songs to God's faithfulness.[16] The psalms were used for worship in the Temple. One hundred fifty in all, they were organized into a hymnal of praise containing five divisions or books, corresponding to the first five books of the Old Testament (The Pentateuch), which included songs of praise, history and prophesy. The psalms teach one to worship reverently; to cultivate intimacy with God; to love, delight in and appreciate God; to conquer foes and find refuge in Him.[17]

As Robert Webber has said, "Through worship, Israel was to maintain its identity as the people of God, for it was in worship that Israel continually recalled and celebrated its relationship to their God."[18] Worship in the Temple was highly organized, but worship would become less formal in the next chapter of Israel's story.

---

16   Vernon M. Whaley, *Called to Worship*, 113.
17   Elmer L. Towns and Vernon M. Whaley, *Worship Through the Ages*, location 597-616.
18   Robert E. Webber, *Worship Old & New*, 23.

Jamie Harvill

WORSHIP IN THE BABYLONIAN EXILE: THE SYNAGOGUE

The coming of the Babylonian Exile (c. 600 BC) was prophesized by Jeremiah (29: 1-14). Israel was once again challenged to find solace in God alone. Still, through difficulty, Israel decided to remain in "comfortable" bondage to other gods, even as Jehovah demanded exclusive allegiance; Israel had forgotten about God's transcendence. As James MacDonald said in his book *Vertical Church*, one must come to the place where in life the quest for comfort and a hassle-free existence must not be one's sole compass and guide. He wrote, "Transcendence helps me accept that there is One who exists outside the boundaries of human knowing, who calls me to bow before Him and serve Him as the true Center of the universe."[19] God shook up the status quo for Israel once again, and they were challenged to respond, even through difficulty and pain.

During the Exile, many of the elite of Israel were captured and brought to Babylon, forcing them to adjust to a new culture and to adopt a new display of worship. The armies of Nebuchadnezzar destroyed the Temple at

---

19   James MacDonald, *Vertical Church: What Every Heart Longs For—What Every Church Can Be* (Colorado Springs, CO: David C. Cook, 2012), Kindle Electronic Edition, chapter 1, location 519.

Jerusalem in 586 BC. Consequently, Israel's former system of worship would cease—for the time being anyway. The Synagogue, or the "gathering place," was developed over time in Babylon to help preserve and propagate the Word of God, and to continue to establish and nurture community among those who were exiled.[20] Worship in the Synagogue stressed prayer, affirmation of faith, and reading of Scripture—the study of the Torah; music was organized and conducted by lay people.[21] Sermons also were offered, and the congregants were helped to apply Scripture to daily life.[22] Worship practices in the Synagogue strongly influenced the early Christian church. Christ would usher in the very fulfillment and actualization of what in the OT Tabernacle and Temple were only figurative depictions of Emmanuel—God With Us.

Worship and the New Covenant: Jesus

Jesus is the ultimate focus of worship, and His coming to earth was to initiate God's desire to dwell among mankind in the flesh. Eventually God would offer His Son Jesus as a sacrifice for forgiveness of sin.

---

20   Robert E. Webber, *Worship Old & New*, 36.
21   Andrew Wilson-Dickson, *The Story of Christian Music*, 22.
22   Ibid., 37-38.

Humanity was responsible for their iniquity and deserved punishment, but Christ agreed to take that punishment upon Himself.[23] At the beginning of His ministry, though, Jesus walked the vicinity of Galilee among everyday people, out of which He would choose twelve disciples, and with whom He would concentrate the last three years of His life—to train, to teach and to employ hands-on ministry.

Jesus is God's complete image of Himself. From even before creation, and until the appointed time would come, all things were directed toward Jesus the Son. So in Jesus, one sees the fulfillment of God's plan of redemption, and with it the believer recognizes what ultimate worship is: To love God with all of one's heart, to worship Him and respond to Him, and to allow that excitement for God to draw others to Him as well.[24]

As for worship in action, Jesus expressed through the Great Commandment (Matt. 22: 37-40) to love God with one's whole heart and to love one's neighbor in the same way they love themselves. He puts feet to that commandment with the Great Commission (Matt. 28:

---

23   Robert H. Thune and Will Walker, *The Gospel-Centered Life* (Greensboro, NC: New Growth Press, 2009), 8-9.
24   Ron Owens, *Return to Worship: A God-Centered Approach* (Nashville: B & H, 1999), 23; 27.

19-20), saying, go into the entire world and make disciples—baptizing, teaching, and mentoring them—and Jesus promises the Holy Spirit will be fully present through it all. With these two directives, there is no question as to the heart of God, that Christ-followers must be totally engaged in *Great Commission worship!*[25]

Although there is no definitive place in the NT to find a set of instructions for rituals of Christian worship, there is, however, indirect or "circumstantial" evidence throughout Scripture from which to create a heartfelt and God-honoring practice of worship. For instance, when Jesus met with His disciples in the Upper Room on the night before He would give Himself away to His captors, Jesus did four things in worship, a few of which may be obscure and easy to miss, but nonetheless they are displays of worship one must consider: (1) Jesus instituted the ordinance of the Lord's Supper; (2) Jesus washed the disciples' feet to remind them that His followers are those who serve one another, not those who expect to be served [Luke 22:24; John 13:8]; (3) Jesus prayed a priestly prayer over the disciples [John 17]; and (4) at the end of it all, Jesus and the disciples sang a hymn together before going to the Mount of Olives

---

25   David Wheeler and Vernon M. Whaley, *Worship and Witness: Becoming a Great Commission Worshiper* (Nashville: Lifeway, 2007), 7.

[Matt. 26: 30]. Communion, teaching, prayer and singing remain central to most services of Christian worship to the present day.

WORSHIP AT PENTECOST

In the wake of Jesus' resurrection, the church experienced its first Awakening—one that would be like no other. When the day of Pentecost came, believers—one hundred twenty in all—gathered together in an upper room to pray. In times before that Jesus had miraculously appeared to them, and they touched, spoke to and worshiped Him. Jesus explained to them that He must depart so the Comforter could come (John 16:7), that the Holy Spirit would dwell inside of their hearts (John 14: 16-17). Once again they were together praying—the building shook this time and they were all filled with the Holy Spirit. They began to speak in other languages, praising God for the great things He had done (Acts 2:2-12). Peter preached and three thousand believed, were baptized and were added to their number (Acts 2: 43-47). The church was born that day, and it was not in a Temple, Synagogue or in a Tabernacle—but in the hearts of men and women. People were now free to worship Jesus in their spirits![26] Worship practices originating during the time of Pentecost are recorded in Acts 2:41-

---

26   Elmer L. Towns and Vernon M. Whaley, *Worship Through the Ages*, location 770.

47, where they are described as:

> ...tasks of teaching (doctrine), sharing (the good news; their testimonies; their possessions; their fellowship), breaking bread (meals; communion; feeding the poor), and praying together (prayers of thanksgiving; praise; worship; blessings; supplications).[27]

Worship In the Early Church

The Apostle Paul, in his epistle to the Romans, wrote of the importance of preaching in the early church (Rom. 1:5,16; 12:1–8; 15:9,18; 16:19), and how worship as a lifestyle was a fundamental practice. Worship was then no longer limited to certain rituals, but individuals could contribute their own spiritual gifts as talents and treasures offered to the Lord.[28]

The early church was strictly congregational and individuals could express themselves freely, in formless fashion[29]—without a prescribed liturgy (a fixed set of formalities used in public worship[30]). They did not even

---

27   Ibid., location 861.
28   Ibid., location 871-889.
29   Donald P. Hustad, *Jubilate II*, 145.
30   Bob Kauflin, *Worship Matters: Leading Others to Encounter the Greatness of God* (Wheaton, IL: Crossway Books, 2008), 153.

rely on professional priests at that point to lead the services.[31] With regard to music in the early church, Paul wrote in Ephesians 5:19 that believers should continue "speaking to one another with psalms, hymns, and songs from the Spirit," that they must sing "and make music from [their] heart to the Lord" (NIV). By the end of the first century, four prominent aspects of worship are present in the church: teaching, sharing, breaking bread, and praying.[32] It also became customary to meet on the first day of the week (Resurrection Day) to observe the Lord's Supper and to eat a meal together called a "love feast."[33]

Christian theology was continually being developed, propagated in Paul's writings and through the teachings of the other apostles. In the book of Hebrews, for instance, foundational doctrine was established, including the concept of Christ as High Priest (Heb. 8); Christ as the ultimate, "once-and-for-all" sacrifice (Heb. 9-10); a call to obedience and thanksgiving (Heb. 12); and the contrast of the Old and New Covenants, with an appeal to offer a continual sacrifice of praise to God through Christ, while doing good and sharing with those

---

31 Ibid., 145.
32 Elmer L. Towns and Vernon M. Whaley, *Worship Through the Ages,* location 934.
33 Donald P. Hustad, *Jubilate II*, 144.

in need (Heb. 13:15). The book of Romans, for example, is Paul's key to understanding the rest of the Bible and how to be "right with God" (Rom. 1:16, 17; 3:21, 22). He wrote to Christians in Rome to help expand their understanding of fruitful Christian living.[34]

Approximately twenty years after Christ's ascension (Acts 15: 13-18), it was proposed that Christianity—the new Jewish sect—would accept Gentiles who sought the Lord, a revolutionary and controversial concept. The persecution of early Christians, including brutal methods used by the Roman emperor Nero, caused the church to disperse from Jerusalem. Roman historian Tacitus wrote that Nero would dress the Christians like animals for amusement to later be killed by dogs. Other martyrs were crucified or burned alive.[35]

---

[34] Warren W. Wiersbe, *Be Right: A practical guide to discover how to be right with God, yourself, and others* (Wheaton, IL: Victor Books, 1977), 5.

[35] Elmer L. Towns and Vernon M. Whaley, *Worship Through the Ages,* location 1049-1058.

Worship in the 2ⁿᵈ and 3ʳᵈ Centuries

It is helpful to use secular histories as testimony to how Christians worshiped in the first centuries of the church. In the case of pagan historian Pliny, through a letter to the Roman emperor Trajan, it was reported that Christians met on a fixed day, early in the morning, and sang hymns to Christ, who they professed as God. They also made oaths to remain holy, and then departed to eat a meal together.[36]

In the *Apology* to the Emperor Antonius Pius (ca. AD 150), Justin Martyr wrote a description of a worship service containing two sections (music was not mentioned): (1) *The Service of the Word*, containing readings, a sermon and common prayers; and (2) *The Service of the Lord's Supper*, including a Kiss of Peace, an offering, a prayer of thanksgiving and communion.[37] In the 3ʳᵈ century, other reports of similar services were made available. These practices of early Christian worship were directly connected to the first believers and their traditions, which have the potential to inform and encourage modern worshipers.

---

36 Donald P. Hustad, *Jubilate II,* 160.
37 Ibid., 160.

The theologian Tertullian is considered to be the "father of Latin theology." Born around AD 150, he confronted heretical theological beliefs—religious viewpoints that were contrary to the fundamental orthodox beliefs (approved teachings) of the church. It is important to note that heretics have served the church in an inadvertent way, particularly in the early days, but even up to the present.[38] Erroneous assertions regarding truth must be strongly confronted, which forces the church to form accurate theology—organized statements of biblical revelation. These officially sanctioned orthodox teachings (doctrines) were then widely embraced by the larger church. So, as a result of diligent, Spirit-led theologians like Tertullian, among others, an orthodox understanding was formed regarding ordinances of the church, including the Lord's Supper and baptism. Tertullian also helped advance an orthodox understanding of the Trinity, and was the first person to use the Latin word *trinitas*, meaning "trinity."[39]

Furthermore, the model of the Trinity is vitally important in forming one's theology of worship.[40] God is a relational being and lives in eternal relationship within

---

38 Dr. Bruce L. Shelley, *Church History in Plain Language: Fourth Edition* (Nashville, Thomas Nelson, 2013), 35; 49.
39 Ibid., 49.
40 Ibid., 36.

Himself as the triune God (1 Cor. 2:10-11; Rom. 8:26-27).[41] This model of fellowship is extended to include the believer's relationship to God, through Christ, in the Spirit, and toward one another, in unity, as a community of faith. Early communities of Christ-followers, having survived virtually underground for three centuries, would soon be catapulted into the mainstream.

On the eve of a major battle, the Roman "master of the empire" Constantine turned to faith in Christ. He then amply defeated his enemies and subsequently, through the Edict of Milan, pronounced acceptance for Christianity in the empire. (AD 313).[42] Now royalty in Rome, according to historian Robert Webber, was "courting the favor of the church." Webber continued, "This worldview shift put the church into a friendly environment where, with gifts of buildings in which to worship, the worship of the church shifted from intimacy to theater."[43] During this time the use of incense—a traditional form of respect toward emperors—became an integral part of orthodox worship. Influenced by royalty, many religious leaders began to wear decorated gar-

---

41   Gordon D. Fee, *Paul, the Spirit, and the People of God* (Grand Rapids, MI: Baker Academic, 1996), 46.
42   Elmer L. Towns and Vernon M. Whaley, *Worship Through the Ages,* Kindle Digital Edition, location 1076.
43   Robert E. Webber, *Old and New*, 95.

ments (vestments), and physical gestures became more ceremonial and elaborate. The formal processional developed out of this royal influence as well.[44]

WORSHIP IN THE 4ᵀᴴ AND 5ᵀᴴ CENTURIES

By the 4th century, worship practices were becoming well formed, and measures were taken to standardize them. By AD 400, the Roman Empire was divided into Western and Eastern Empires, and the royal court at Constantinople was pushing for uniformity in worship in order to strengthen political bonds between the two—thus creating strict orthodox practices.[45]

The 4th century Laodicean Council (c. AD 350)—a gathering of church officials who assembled to discuss and settle matters of doctrine and practice—made this decree: "If laymen are forbidden to preach and interpret the Scriptures, much more are they forbidden to sing publicly in church."[46] This effectually silenced congregational worship in the church for the next ten centuries.

---

44 Justo L. Gonzales, *The History of Christianity, Volume 1: The Early Church to the Dawn of the Reformation* (San Francisco: Harper and Row, 1985), 125.

45 Donald P. Hustad, *Jubilate II,* 166.

46 Elmer L. Towns and Vernon M. Whaley, *Worship Through the Ages,* Kindle Edition, location 1590.

Also, due to royal influence, the worship leader became a priest, and the congregation—once participants—increasingly became observers of worship. The erroneous concept of transubstantiation—where the bodily presence of Christ was believed to actually be present in the elements—was well developed by this time.[47]

WORSHIP IN THE MEDIEVAL PERIOD

The Medieval Period (AD 500-1500)—also known as the *Middle Ages* or the *Dark Ages*—witnessed great church growth. But while the church may have claimed more converts, discipleship weakened as ministers adapted to accommodate the overwhelming load.[48]

Monasticism (from the Greek monachos, the root for monk, a word meaning "alone") was a religious way of life in which one renounced worldly interests to dedicate oneself fully to spiritual work. This became an early reaction to perceived spiritual exploitation in the growing church. Pope Gregory (540-604) became known for his Gregorian chants, drawn from the Jew-

---

[47] Donald P. Hustad, *Jubilate II,* 165.
[48] Elmer L. Towns and Vernon M. Whaley, *Worship Through the Ages,* Kindle Edition, location 1296.

ish Synagogue.[49] Certain monks, including St. Benedict (c. 480-c. 547) and St. Francis of Assisi (1182-1226), became namesakes for communities, or orders, that were guided by particular religious rules that they followed. The innovation of written notation came about during the Middle Ages. Where previously music required memorization, and was sung and passed on from generation to generation by oral tradition, an Italian Benedictine monk named Guido of Arezzo (995-1033) is credited as the inventor of what has since developed into the modern system of music notation.[50]

One of the most significant events of the church came in 1054 when Western and Eastern Christendom split—an event theologians and historians call the Great Schism. The church at Rome (Western) and the other centered in Constantinople (Eastern) were regularly at odds concerning disputes over conflicting claims of church authority, and aspects of the Nicene creed, which culminated in a separation. Due to the break by the Western Church, many in the Eastern Orthodox Church (Greek speaking) claim theirs to be the original church—declaring her history can be traced in unbroken continuity all the way back to Christ and the twelve apostles.

---

49   Ibid., location 1369.
50   Ibid., location 1409.

With the Reformation forthcoming, another schism would again alter the church and worship.

WORSHIP AND THE REFORMATION

The 16th century was a time of great turmoil, and with the Renaissance (4th–17th centuries), individualism was on the rise. All the while, unnecessary church traditions and a desire for more freedom in worship created a profound desire for ecclesiastical and theological reform.[51] The Roman Catholic Church had become so corrupt that on October 31, 1517, a brave Augustinian monk named Martin Luther (1483-1546) from Wittenberg, Germany, posted ninety-five theses (arguments) to the door of the church at Wittenberg Castle. The complaint challenged teachings of the Catholic Church regarding the nature of penance (obtaining forgiveness from a priest), the authority of the pope and the usefulness of indulgences (usually a monetary remission for sin).[52] Because of the recent invention of the printing press, pamphlets of Luther's arguments were distributed. Making their way around Europe within a month,

---

51 Robert E. Webber, *Worship Old and New*, 109.
52 Theopedia, "95 Theses," http://www.theopedia.com/95-theses (accessed August 10, 2015).

the leaflets helped garner widespread support for the rogue priest.[53]

The Catholic Church spared Luther death as a heretic, while several other displaced critics of the Church also came to light, including Swiss reformers John Calvin (1509-1564) and Ulrich Zwingli (1484-1531), and eventually England's Henry VIII (1491-1547). These rebel leaders were referred to as Reformers and, along with their congregants, were also known as Protestants. The Reformed community unanimously rejected doctrines of transubstantiation. They desired that the Word of God be returned to its former prominence in worship, and for worship to be in the vernacular (language) of the people. Also, with the exception of Zwingli, the Reformers desired to return to the two-fold structure of Word and sacrament.[54]

Luther was not only known for his theology, but also for his songwriting. He believed songs should be understandable enough to learn by heart, thus they should be simple—familiar to ordinary people.[55] He wrote both <u>melody and ly</u>rics, and was known as a vocalist and

[53] Andrew Wilson-Dickson, *The Story of Christian Music*, 58.

[54] Robert E. Webber, *Worship Old and New*, 111.

[55] Ibid., 63.

41

guitarist. He believed more people were won to Christ through his singing than his preaching.[56]

John Calvin, a songwriter himself, had a strong conviction that the text used for hymns in worship must come directly from Scripture, particularly the Psalms.[57] Each of the Reformers believed in *Free Worship*, as opposed to the constraints of the Catholic Mass. *Free worship* is a distinctive characteristic of modern-day evangelical worship— described as non-liturgical—without a fixed order. Many churches that are liturgical in nature have adapted free worship practices in the musical portion of the service, due to the influence of charismatic worship along with praise and worship song offerings.[58]

A quick overview of Protestant worship suggests that: (1) worship return to the classic liturgies in the spirit of the Church Fathers; (2) that congregants be able to comprehend the meaning and significance of each component of worship, with an authentic desire to experience God; and (3) that worship be substantive as well as practical.[59]

---

56 Elmer L. Towns and Vernon M. Whaley, *Worship Through the Ages,* Kindle Edition, location 1600.

57 Ibid., location 1605-1618.

58 Donald P. Hustad, *Jubilate II,* xix.

59 Robert E. Webber, *Worship Old and New*, 119.

Records show that in 1608 Holland, a service in an Anabaptist church would start with prayer, a Scripture would be read, and then another prayer, a sermon would be preached based on a biblical text, the congregation was given an opportunity to speak, followed by another prayer, and finally an offering was given.[60]

DIVERSE WORSHIP

Thanks to the Reformation, by the 1600s European hymn writers were prolific. But for one thousand years leading up to the Reformation, hymn singing was a dangerous occupation. Jan Hus (c. 1370-1415), an early Reformer from modern-day Prague, began to write hymns in his own tongue. His boldness in publically singing hymns, and for promoting early reformed ideals such as "priesthood of all believers," led to his being burned at the stake by the Catholic Church. In the following century, great hymn writing would increase in Germany through Luther, Calvin, the Moravians, Von Zinzendorf, along with notables like J. S. Bach.[61] English hymns were being crafted in Reformed England through

---

60   Donald P. Hustad, *Jubilate II*, 201.

61   Robert J. Morgan, *Then Sings My Soul: The Story of Our Songs—Drawing Strength from the Great Hymns of Our Faith, Book 3* (Nashville: Thomas Nelson, 2011), 31-36.

the likes of Isaac Watts, the Wesleys, Newton, Cowper and the blind and crippled Charlotte Elliott, who wrote "Just As I Am."[62]

Much like the training that commenced during the Praise and Worship Movement of the late-20th century, singing schools in the 18th century had a major impact on congregational singing. Many Americans learned doctrine and theology from hymns that the overseas Protestant songwriters were creating. Singing schools gave opportunity for American hymn writers to compose, using indigenous melodies like those originating from the mountains of Appalachia.[63]

---

62   Ibid., 37-46.
63   Elmer L. Towns and Vernon M. Whaley, *Worship Through the Ages,* locations 1877-1885.

WORSHIP AND THE AWAKENINGS IN EUROPE AND AMERICA

The gospel traveled to America's eastern seaboard by way of the revivals in Europe, including the preaching of Englishman, John Wesley (1703-1791). Meanwhile, the universities of New England were being transformed under the influence of Timothy Dwight, Nathaniel Taylor and Bishop Francis Asbury. The revival moved to places inland, carrying the message of Christ to the rugged, independent folk of Kentucky, where the great Camp Meetings were held, led by common people like the humble itinerant Methodist preacher, Peter Cartwright.

James McGready (1763-1817) led the Cane Ridge Revival of 1801 and thousands came to Christ. Two years later, the term "camp meeting" came into common use, referring to the outdoor venues, tents, and meals cooked over an open flame. Far from the Enlightenment establishment of Britain and New England, by 1811 the undereducated ploughboy preachers of the Kentucky wilderness had organized more than 400 camps.[64] The number of both Methodists and Baptists grew rapidly.

---

64 Elmer L. Towns and Vernon M. Whaley, *Worship Through the Ages,* location 2139, Kindle Edition.

Circuit preachers came into form during this time, defined as a single preacher serving multiple congregations over great distances.

During the Camp Meeting Awakening (1727-1790), people began to express themselves with greater emotion and bodily movement. The camp atmosphere helped encourage multi ethnic worship, and folk music and spirituals were being sung.[65] In the years following the American Revolution, the United States experienced an extended phase of spiritual decline.[66] Revival on American soil helped the new nation find a fresh spiritual path. Throughout the spiritual history of the United States, it has been by way of natural disasters, wars and other tragedies that Americans would again turn to God for strength and comfort. Worship practices would also continue to develop through subsequent centuries of societal change.

---

65   Ibid., locations 2204-2236.
66   Ibid., location 1983.

WORSHIP AND THE GREAT REVIVALS OF THE 19ᵀᴴ THROUGH THE 21ˢᵀ CENTURIES

The Sunday School Revivals in England, which had spilled over to America (1820-1850), influenced great songwriters like Francis Scott Key (1779-1843)—writer of the American National Anthem—who by the 1830s became president of the American Sunday School Union. This era also witnessed the immense influence of lawyer-turned-revivalist, Charles Grandison Finney (1792-1876).

Finney and his music partner, Thomas Hastings (1784-1872), transformed worship, asserting that evangelism, rather than worship, was the priority of the church. Finney also retrofitted sanctuaries to maximize the need for suitable ministry stations during revival services. His meetings would go on for weeks, even months at a time. Finney popularized the "invitation" or "altar call" at the end of his services—a practice still found in many evangelical worship services today. Simple, easy-to-sing songs came from this period—Sunday school songs that declared the joys of heaven, the love of Christ, and the satisfaction of the Christian life.[67]

---

67   Ibid., location 2450.

The Laymen's Prayer Revival was a grassroots prayer movement (1857-1890). During this period, in October of 1871, the great Chicago Fire ravaged the city, claiming more than three hundred lives and leaving one hundred thousand people homeless. This event prompted Dwight. L. Moody (1837-1899)—a former shoe salesman and Sunday school teacher-turned-pastor—to preach the gospel in evangelistic meetings. Throughout his ministry—along with worship leader, Ira Sankey (1840-1908)—Moody transformed "worship evangelism."[68] Sankey was known for his significant use of choirs, simple gospel songs and use of testimonies in the meetings. Some even accused the duo of a lack of reverence in their revival meeting settings.[69] During this period, songwriters such as Fanny Crosby, Philip Phillips, Philip Bliss, Frances Havergal and Lina Sandrell-Berg were all making contributions to the hymnody of the church.[70]

At the turn of the 20th century, and after the great San Francisco Earthquake of 1906, African American preacher William Seymour was speaking on Sunday April 14th of that same year that some had proclaimed the end of the world was at hand. The Holy Spirit fell

68	Ibid., location 2743.
69	Ibid., location 2753.
70	Ibid., locations 2802-2839.

on that congregation at 321 Azusa Street in Los Angeles, and tremendous revival began, helping to launch the Pentecostal Movement (Azusa Revival 1906-c.1915). Along with multiethnic worship, Seymour's meetings focused on speaking in tongues, miracles, anointing with oil and healing, prophetic utterances with interpretation, along with great expressions of emotion during the lengthy services.[71]

African American jazz piano player, Thomas A. Dorsey (1899-1993), was influenced by traditional gospel music when evangelist Billy Sunday (1862-1935) and his musical partner, Homer Rodeheaver (1880-1955), visited Dorsey's hometown of Atlanta, Georgia, to conduct a crusade. During one of those meetings the young Dorsey committed his musical talent to the Lord. After spending some years as a blues musician, he would eventually come back to ministry to invent the black choir sound, and introduce percussion and handclapping into worship. By the end of his life he would compose over one thousand songs, two of which were "Peace In the Valley" and "Precious Lord, Take My Hand."[72] During this time of great revival, soloists began to join with choirs during worship services. Gospel music was be-

---

71 Ibid., location 3350.
72 Ibid., location 3603 and 3630.

coming popular, and several forms of white gospel and black gospel music were transforming worship. These musical styles utilized simple lyrics, personal testimony, along with accompaniment that was joyful and amusing.

Post-WWII America ushered in the Baby Boom Generation (1946-1964). This would lead to great revival in the younger segment of society with Billy Graham's influence, including organizations such as Youth for Christ, Inter Varsity Christian Fellowship, and Campus Crusade for Christ.

Billy Graham (1918-) is a prominent modern-day personality who made abundant use of media in his evangelistic efforts. He contributed much to the spread of the gospel following WWII with use of radio, television and other methods that became a staple for mass communication.[73]

The Bible College Movement of the '50s and '60s helped mobilize ministers and music directors into the field to reach the nation and world for Christ.[74] Musicians such as Ralph Carmichael (1927-) and George Beverly Shea (1909-2013) would contribute to choral

---

73 Ibid., location 4650.
74 Ibid., location 4034.

and revival music coming from the Graham Crusades. Radio and television became a great avenue for evangelism and gospel music presentation. Now, people could choose to stay home with great front-row views of the nation's best preachers, teachers, music groups and crusades.

In the late 1960s, Chuck Smith (1927-2013), pastor of Calvary Chapel in Costa Mesa, California, through the prompting of the Hoy Spirit—and with great prodding from his wife—reached out to the hippie population hanging around the beaches near the church. His preaching and love for those counter-culture, barefooted and unkempt young people drew thousands to be converted and baptized right there on the beach. This led to the fusion of popular rock music with a Christian message, and it began to be used in worship services that Chuck was opening to the new hippie converts (initially, much to the dismay of several older members of Calvary Chapel).[75] This period contributed to what became known as the Jesus Movement (1960-1985).

Billy Graham's influence on the Jesus Movement, also known as the Jesus People Movement, was rooted in his utilizing secular performers for evangelistic

---

75   Ibid., location 4308-4333.

purposes. With the groundbreaking *Explo '72*, Graham invited popular music stars to join him in his crusades, including the likes of Kris Kristofferson and Johnny and June Cash. This six-day event, held at the Cotton Bowl in Dallas, Texas, helped integrate the Jesus Movement into mainstream American Christianity.[76]

Chuck Smith created a music company to record and distribute music from groups and individuals emerging from the Jesus Movement and Calvary Chapel; Maranatha! Music was born in 1971. Smith's nephew, Chuck Fromm, was later asked to lead the company in 1975. This Baby Boomer revival, which subsequently initiated Contemporary Christian Music (CCM), helped pave the way for the Praise and Worship Awakening (1985-2000). Pop-styled praise music would be distributed to churches across the world, through companies such as Maranatha! Music, Integrity Music, Worship Together, Passion, Hillsong and Vineyard Music, to name a few. In his award-winning book about the Jesus Movement, and of the significant spiritual revolution in post-WWII America, Larry Eskridge writes:

> This pop culture–friendly aspect of the Jesus People movement had tremendous implications

---

76   Ibid., location 4364.

for the role of music within the evangelical subculture. First, the Jesus People's enthusiasm for pop and rock music-based idioms brought forth Jesus Rock and, in so doing, marked the beginnings of what would eventually become the Contemporary Christian Music (CCM) industry, which has become a major component of American evangelicalism's mass media and bookstore infrastructure, as well as a significant aspect of everyday life and devotion, spawning radio station formats, summer festivals, Web sites, and the like.[77]

POSTMODERNISM AND THE FUTURE OF WORSHIP IN THE CHURCH

To properly understand worship and the church over the centuries, one must recognize the powerful influence that cultural change has brought to each era's understanding of God and the world. It is widely understood that Western civilization may be divided into three basic chronological periods, thus revealing the dominant philosophies of each era, which are known as *Premodern* (beginning of history to roughly 1650),

---

[77] Larry Eskridge, *Gods Forever Family: The Jesus People Movement in America* (New York: Oxford University Press, 2013), 8.

Modern (1650-1960) and *Postmodern* (1960-present).

Citizens of the *Premodern* period believed truth to be absolute, based upon revealed knowledge from authoritative and unopposed sources—ultimately considered to originate from God. The Catholic Church flourished during this period. *Modernism* then characterized a shift from ecclesiastical and governmental sources of authority to empiricism (understanding through the senses), modern science, reason and logic. This three hundred-year period, which included the Enlightenment—a European intellectual movement of the 17th and 18th centuries—was preoccupied with open-minded progress. In the Enlightenment, man's primary concern was not heaven but happiness and fulfillment in the here and now; and that reason, not faith, was the greatest method to achieve happiness, not "emotions, or myths, or superstitions."[78] The foundation of this philosophy, though, was shaken by the inhumanity displayed during the holocaust of World War II. Emanating from Modernism was awareness that civilization had not evolved, that there was no apparent progress over time toward increased compassion regarding suffering and injustice.[79]

---

[78] Dr. Bruce L. Shelley, *Church History in Plain Language*, 324.

Consequently, the *postmodern* mindset developed out of dissatisfaction with what Modernism promised but did not deliver—a better future.[80] Of the transition to postmodernity, theologian and teacher Marva Dawn explains:

> Instead of trusting authorities, human beings insisted increasingly on their autonomy, and all truth, including what could be scientifically determined, became relative. Now God was no longer absolute, and religion was marginalized to the private sphere. People could simply say, 'Christianity might be true for you, but it is not true for me.'[81]

---

79   Dominick LaCapra, "Modernism, Postmodernism, and Rationality after the Holocaust," (interview by Amos Goldberg, conducted on June 9, 1998, for the Shoah Resource Center of The International School for Holocaust Studies, Jerusalem), http://www.yadvashem.org/odot_pdf/Microsoft%20Word%20-%203865.pdf (accessed December 30, 2015).

80   David F. Wells, *Above All Earthly Pow'rs: Christ in a Postmodern World* (Grand Rapids: William. B. Eerdmans Publishing, 2006), 67.

81   Marva J. Dawn, *A Royal Waste of Time: The Splendor of Worshiping God and Being Church for the World* (Grand Rapids, MI: William B. Eerdmans Publishing Co., 1999), locations 519-521, Kindle Edition.

The postmodern interpretation of truth is both deeply subjective and profoundly relative; truth is based on who perceives it.[82] Therefore, Christianity is highly suspect among many in this present age,[83] and being a Christian today can be dangerous in light of anti-Christian sentiments. The late Charles Colson once said, "Tolerance has become so important that no exception is tolerated."[84]

Even as Christianity becomes increasingly sidelined in popular culture, God's truth has not diminished. The Bible is the inspired, inerrant and infallible Word of God; it has been preserved by Him, and is the final authority in all matters of doctrine and faith, above all human authority (Isa. 40:8; Ps. 12:6-7; 18:30; 119:105; 119:160, Matt. 5:18; Matt 24:35; John 17:17; 2 Tim. 3:16; Heb. 4:12; 2 Pet. 1:20-21; 2 Pet. 3:15-16).[85] The Bible contains a never-changing set of principles applicable for all people in every age. Even as history and societ-

---

82 Robb Redman, *The Great Worship Awakening: Singing a New Song in the Postmodern Church* (San Francisco: Josey-Bass, 2002), 134-135.

83 Richard Rorty and Gianni Vattimo, *The Future of Religion* (New York, NY: Columbia University Press, 2005), 33.

84 Charles Colson and Nan Pearcey, *How Now Shall We Live?* (Wheaton, IL: Tyndale, 1999), 23.

85 "What Evangelical Christians Believe," http://evangelicalbeliefs.com/ (accessed January 2, 2016).

ies supposedly advance, the good news of the gospel remains as steadfast and pertinent in the 21st century as it was in the 1st century (2 Tim. 3:16-17; Rev. 1:8).[86] "The harder and faster the church runs after God (via the truth)," says pastor and author Jeffrey Johnson, "the brighter its spiritual illumination will shine in this unholy and secular world."[87]

Tim Keller—author and pastor of a thriving church in the heart of New York City—has a unique view of the complex cultural and spiritual landscape that has been developing in America and the world over the past one hundred years. He also submits observations about the half-century of postmodernism's philosophical dominance by pointing out that there is neither the "Western Christendom of the past nor the secular, religionless society that was predicted for the future."[88] Keller observes that what is present is something altogether different. Ironically, both religious belief and skepticism are on

---

[86] Glenn Pearson, *That's a Great Question: What to Say When Your Faith Is Questioned* (Colorado Springs, CO: David C. Cook, 2010), 14.

[87] Jeffrey D. Johnson, *The Church: Why Bother?: The Nature, Purpose, & Functions of the Local Church* (Conway, AR: Free Grace Press, 2015), locations 703-705, Kindle Edition.

[88] Timothy Keller, *The Reason for God: Belief in an Age of Skepticism* (New York: Penguin Publishing Group, 2008), location 165, Kindle Edition.

the increase.[89] But inescapable in North American culture is a tendency to be *spiritual* but *non-religious* at the same time.

Issues about modern-day commercialism, popular music and amusement influencing the church and worship today must be examined. Questions to ask may include: Will Postmoderns be able to discover worship practices in churches with an awareness of the reality and presence of God that postmodernity cannot provide? Can evangelical churches effectively experience components of mystery, of sacrament, of the "the deeper resonances of ritual action to connect with this postmodern sensibility?"[90] It is therefore essential that a robust theology of worship be studied, communicated and practiced in churches, for today's worshiper and for future believers. Tom Rainer submits that Millennials (persons reaching young adulthood around the year 2000) are looking for worship music with rich theological content, authenticity and quality of delivery, based on prayerful preparation.[91] It is interesting to note the

---

[89] Ibid.

[90] John Jefferson Davis, *Worship and the Reality of God: An Evangelical Theology of Real Presence* (Downers Grove, IL: IVP Academic, 2010), location 851-855, Kindle Edition.

[91] Thom S. Rainer, "What Worship Style Attracts the Millennials?" (April 2, 2014), http://thomrainer.com/2014/04/worship-style-attracts-millennials/ (accessed December 29, 2015).

similarities in what Millennials of the 21st century long for and what the 16th century Reformers sought to recapture in worship.

A recent article proposed that "contemporary" worship is in decline. In the critique, Jonathan Aigner stressed reasons for its demise, a few of which include the reality that (1) Baby Boomers—the driving force of CCM—are losing their influence; (2) that Millennials are seeking old ways of doing things—more emphasis is being placed on liturgy and less on using music as an attraction for evangelistic purposes; and (3) that the term 'contemporary worship' requires an unquestioning loyalty to "the new, the current, the hip, the cool, and the commercial."[92] Aigner asserts that worship must not be about archaic vs. new, old vs. young, and certainly must not be about taste, for music only plays a part. Worship ultimately is about believers gathering together to glorify Christ. And therefore, to that end, worship practices must also be about ancient and future, not just about here and now.[93]

---

92 Jonathan Aigner, "3 Reasons Contemporary Worship IS Declining, and What We Can Do to Help the Church Move On," http://www.patheos.com/blogs/ponderanew/2015/09/04/3-reasons-contemporary-worship-is-declining-and-5-things-we-can-do-to-help-the-church-move-on/ (accessed December 29, 2015).
93 Ibid.

Conclusion

With the study of worship from creation to the 21st century, many things come to bear, including the reality that worship styles will continually be in process—*Semper Reformanda,* which in Latin means "always evolving and reforming." Because there is no set order for worship found in the New Testament, Christ-followers in each generation and culture have been able to worship freely and creatively in spirit and truth (John 4: 24). It is also evident that worship has ebbed and flowed *into* and *out of* the hands of everyday, ordinary worshipers. The tendency has been to formalize worship, to give it to professionals to handle, when all along Scripture has simply called the church to draw near to God and to encourage each believer in the faith (Heb. 10:22). Congregational singing has been significant in the history of worship, along with preaching, reading Scripture, prayer and Communion. True worship ultimately empowers believers to collectively celebrate the gospel of Jesus Christ—the good news of salvation.

Worship must originate and grow out of an intense desire to know and love God in all His fullness.[94]

---

[94] Vernon M. Whaley, *The Dynamics of Corporate Worship* (Grand Rapids, MI: Baker Books, 2001), 23.

A. W. Tozer spoke of returning to the essence of worship when he wrote:

> The purpose of God in sending His Son to die and rise and live and be at the right hand of God the Father was that He might restore to us the missing jewel, the jewel of worship; that we might come back and learn to do again that which we were created to do in the first place – worship the Lord in the beauty of holiness, to spend our time in awesome wonder and adoration of God, feeling and expressing it, and letting it get into our labors and doing nothing except as an act of worship to Almighty God through His Son, Jesus Christ.[95]

Even as styles and expressions continue to evolve, biblical principles must be employed to govern worship practices. As previously stated, Scripture teaches that the church must worship in spirit and in truth (John 4: 24). Worship must also be Christ-centered and not man-centered (Matt. 4:10; Rom. 15:1-7; Heb. 13:15). The Word of God must guide worship (Ps. 119:105; 2 Tim. 3:16-17), and worship must be a holy and sacred endeavor, an activity strengthened with purity of heart

---

[95] A. W. Tozer, *Whatever Happened to Worship: A Call to True Worship* (Camp Hill, PA: Wing Spread Publishers, 2012), 129.

and mind (Ps. 66:18; John 5:24; 1 Thess. 5:22). Congregational worship must be orderly (1 Cor. 14: 26-33); it must be thoughtfully and skillfully employed as an encouragement to the congregation, with clearly communicated content and musical sing-ability, because worship also edifies and instructs the Body of Christ (Eph. 5:19; Col. 3:16).[96] Through worship, Christ-followers publically exhibit the reality that they are an earthly "colony of heaven," of which an unbelieving world can behold what heaven is to be like, and how its citizens can lovingly live in community and in purity.[97]

If the church endeavors to aim for and pursue this end, God's people will experience true fulfillment for which they were designed (Eph. 4:1-16). The call to worship resonates throughout the centuries in the Great Commandment that Jesus spoke before He left the earth, and it will bring blessing to all who obey:

> You shall love the Lord your God with all your heart, and with all your soul, and with all your mind. This is the great and first commandment. And a second is like it, You shall love your neighbor as yourself. On these two commandments

---

[96] Jeffrey D. Johnson, *The Church: Why Bother,* locations 884-988.

[97] Gordon D. Fee, *Paul, the Spirit, and the People of God,* 124.

depend all the law and the prophets (Matt. 22: 37-39, RSV).

As previously examined, the Great Commission (Matt. 28: 16-20) is twofold: God's people are sent into the world to *proclaim* salvation and to *serve* the needy. But as Jesus in Matthew 22: 37-39 commands, the church is also called to *worship* and *learn* of Him. Therefore, it is vitally important for believers to consider that "mission without worship can produce empty service, just as worship without mission can lead to careless religion."[98] Discipleship is about cultivating worshiping, obedient, reproducing disciples,[99] with worship as the divine goal of God's redemptive work. It may be difficult for some to understand, but salvation is not an end in itself: *the praise of God* is the ultimate purpose for salvation and evangelism. To grasp this important truth of the priority of worship, one can turn to to Ephesians 1: 11-14, where Paul emphasizes that the purpose for all activity of the church is ultimately to praise God:

> In him we have obtained an inheritance, having been predestined according to the purpose of

---

[98] Dr. Bruce L. Shelley, *Church History in Plain Language*, 382.

[99] David Wheeler and Vernon M. Whaley, *Worship and Witness: Becoming a Great Commission Worshiper,* location 2219.

him who works all things according to the counsel of his will, so that we who were the first to hope in Christ might be *to the praise of his glory.* In him you also, when you heard the word of truth, the gospel of your salvation, and believed in him, were sealed with the promised Holy Spirit, who is the guarantee of our inheritance until we acquire possession of it, *to the praise of his glory* (ESV, italics added).

The purpose for life, the motivation for hope, and the reason that the Word has been freely given is to glorify and worship God. The goal of salvation, and for the seal of promise—the guarantee of each believer's inheritance in Christ, through the Holy Spirit—is for God's glory. The ultimate work of the church is to bring glory to God (Rom. 16: 25-27).

May Christ be worshiped, adored, lifted up, exalted and praised through His church, and may the high honor and priority of worshiping Him be biblically and skillfully propagated to successive generations for ages to come and into eternity. May God be the glory forever and ever, AMEN!

BIBLIOGRAPHY

Aigner, Jonathan. "3 Reasons Contemporary Worship Is Declining, and What We Can Do to Help the Church Move On," http://www.patheos.com/blogs/ponderanew/2015/09/04/3-reasons-contemporary-worship-is-declining-and-5-things-we-can-do-to-help-the-church-move-on/ (accessed December 29, 2015).

Allen, Ronald B. *The Wonder of Worship*. Nashville: Word Publishing, 2000.

Colson, Charles and Nan Pearcey. *How Now Shall We Live?* Wheaton, IL: Tyndale, 1999.

Davis, John Jefferson. *Worship and the Reality of God: An Evangelical Theology of Real Presence.* Downers Grove, IL: IVP Academic, 2010. Kindle Edition.

Dawn, Marva J. *A Royal Waste of Time: The Splendor of Worshiping God and Being Church for the World*. Grand Rapids, MI: William B. Eerdmans Publishing Co., 1999. Kindle Edition.

Dickson, Andrew Wilson. *The Story of Christian Music: From the Gregorian Chant to Black Gospel—An Illustrated Guide to All the Major Traditions of Music in Worship*. Oxford, England, UK: Lion Books, 1992.

Eskridge, Larry. *Gods Forever Family: The Jesus People Movement in America*. New York: Oxford University Press, 2013.

Fee, Gordon D. *Paul, the Spirit, and the People of God*. Grand Rapids, MI: Baker Academic, 1996.

Gonzales, Justo L. *The History of Christianity, Volume

1: The Early Church to the Dawn of the Reformation. San Francisco: Harper and Row, 1985.

Hill, Andrew E. *Enter His Courts with Praise: Old Testament Worship for the New Testament Church*. Grand Rapids: Baker Books, 1993.

Hustad, Donald P. *Jubilate II: Church Music in Worship and Renewal*. Carol Stream, IL: Hope, 1993.

Jewish Practice, Chabad.org., "An Overview of the Shema," http://www.chabad.org/library/article_cdo/aid/862695/jewish/An-Overview.htm (accessed August 10, 2015).

Johnson, Jeffrey D. *The Church: Why Bother?: The Nature, Purpose, & Functions of the Local Church*. Conway, AR: Free Grace Press, 2015. Kindle Edition.

Kauflin, Bob. *Worship Matters: Leading Others to Encounter the Greatness of God.* Wheaton, IL: Crossway Books, 2008.

Keller, Timothy. *The Reason for God: Belief in an Age of Skepticism.* New York: Penguin Publishing Group, 2008. Kindle Edition.

LaCapra, Dominick. "Modernism, Postmodernism, and Rationality after the Holocaust," (interview by Amos Goldberg, conducted on June 9, 1998, for the Shoah Resource Center of The International School for Holocaust Studies, Jerusalem), http://www.yadvashem.org/odot_pdf/Microsoft%20Word%20-%203865.pdf (accessed December 30, 2015).

Owens, Ron. *Return to Worship: A God-Centered Approach.* Nashville: B&H Publishers, 1999.

Pearson, Glenn. *That's a Great Question: What to*

Say When Your Faith Is Questioned. Colorado Springs, CO: David C. Cook, 2010.

MacDonald, James. *Vertical Church: What Every Heart Longs For—What Every Church Can Be*. Colorado Springs, CO: David C. Cook, 2012. Kindle Edition.

Mathena, Gary M., DMin. *One Thing Needful: An Invitation to the Study of Worship*. Bloomington, IN: CrossBooks, 2013.

Morgan, Robert. *Then Sings My Soul, Book 3*. Nashville: Thomas Nelson, 2011.

Rainer, Thom S. "What Worship Style Attracts the Millennials?" (April 2, 2014). http://thomrainer.com/2014/04/worship-style-attracts-millennials/ (accessed December 29, 2015).

Rorty, Richard and Gianni Vattimo. *The Future of Religion*. New York, NY: Columbia University Press, 2005.

Shelley, Dr. Bruce L. *Church History in Plain Language: Fourth Edition*. Nashville, Thomas Nelson, 2013.

Theopedia, "95 Theses," http://www.theopedia.com/95-theses. (accessed August 10, 2015).

Thune, Robert H. and Will Walker. *The Gospel-Centered Life*. Greensboro, NC: New Growth Press, 2009.

Towns, Elmer L. and Vernon M. Whaley. *Worship Through the Ages: How the Great Awakenings Shape Evangelical Worship*. Nashville: B&H Publications, 2012. Kindle Edition.

Tozer, A. W. *Whatever Happened to Worship: A Call to*

True Worship. Revised Edition. Camp Hill, PA: Wing Spread Publishers, 2012.

Webber, Robert E. *Worship Old and New*. Revised Edition. Nashville: Zondervan, 1994.

Wells, David F. *Above All Earthly Pow'rs: Christ in a Postmodern World*. Grand Rapids: William. B. Eerdmans Publishing, 2006.

Whaley, Vernon M. *Called To Worship: The Biblical Foundations of Our Response to God's Call*. Nashville: Thomas Nelson, 2012.

Whaley, Vernon M. *The Dynamics of Corporate Worship.* Grand Rapids, MI: Baker Books, 2001.

"What Evangelical Christians Believe." http://evangelicalbeliefs.com/ (accessed January 2, 2016).

Wheeler, David and Vernon M. Whaley. *Worship and Witness: Becoming a Great Commission Worshiper*. Nashville: Lifeway, 2012.

Wiersbe, Warren W. *Be Right: A practical guide to discover how to be right with God, yourself, and others*. Wheaton, IL: Victor Books, 1977.

Wiersbe, Warren W. *Real Worship: It Will Transform Your Life*. Nashville: Oliver Nelson Books, 1986.

Study Questions

INTRODUCTION

1. What is mankind's ultimate purpose?

2. If you were to create a definition of worship, what would it be?

3. Of what importance is worship to the church?

4. What is *genuine* worship, according to Andrew Hill?

WORSHIP AND THE OLD COVENANT: ABRAHAM, MOSES AND JOSHUA

1. Which attributes regarding worship were evident in the life of Abraham?

2. List the five basic structural elements for a meet-

ing between God and man that were initiated in Moses' encounter?

3. Which attributes regarding worship were evident in the life of Moses?

4. Which attributes regarding worship were evident in the life of Joshua?

5. The Commander of the Lord's Army, described in Joshua 5:14, is believed to be which person?

6. How did both Moses and Joshua similarly show reverence toward God?

Worship and the Temple

1. According to 1 Kings 5:3, what was God's reason for not allowing David to build the Temple?

2. From which tribe did the musicians and singers who lead worship in the Temple originate?

3. How many chapters are in the book of Psalms? How many divisions are there? List the different types of psalms.

4. Describe in your own words the purpose, according to Robert Webber, for which Israel worshiped.

5. Was worship in the Temple casual or highly organized?

Worship in the Babylonian Exile

1. When did the Babylonian Exile occur and what happened to Israel during this period?

2. When was the Temple destroyed and by whom?

3. For what reason did the synagogue come to be?

4. Describe worship in the synagogue?

5. What are some of the similarities of worship in the synagogue and the modern church?

Worship and the New Covenant: Jesus

1. According to Matthew 22: 37-40, what does Jesus consider "worship in action?"

2. Describe the Great Commission (Matt. 28: 19-20).

3. Is there a singular place in the New Testament for one to find a definitive set of instructions for rituals of Christian worship? Why do you suppose this is true?

4. What was the final thing Jesus and the disciples did before leaving the Upper Room and the Last

Supper?

5. After observing Christ's ministry with the disciples during the Last Supper, which component of worship practiced there is almost non-existent today? Why do you think this is so?

Worship at Pentecost

1. When was the church initiated?

2. For what is Pentecost also known?

3. How many were added to the church at Pentecost?

4. Where was the church actually "born?"

5. What are some of the worship practices found in Acts 2:41-47 that originated at Pentecost?

Worship In the Early Church

1. What was the aspect of worship that Paul em-

phasized in Romans, and what reasons did Paul give for its significance (Rom. 1:16)?

2. What is liturgy? Did the early church use one?

3. List four of the foundational doctrines presented in Hebrews.

4. What was the "revolutionary and controversial concept" introduced to the early church?

5. What happened to many Christians in the early church at the hands of the government, and what was the subsequent result?

Worship in the 2ND and 3RD Centuries

1. How does secular history aid in the understand-

ing of early worship practices?

2. Describe how heretics can possibly "help" the church.

3. How does a proper understanding of the Trinity contribute to biblical worship?

4. What was Constantine's contribution to the church?

5. What were the changes in worship due to Constantine's influence?

Worship in the 4th and 5th Centuries

1. List two factions of the Roman Empire that ex-

isted by AD 400

2. What was the nature of worship practiced during the 4th and 5th centuries?

3. Which major decision was made, and by whom, that would effect worship for the next 1,000 years?

4. How did royalty influence worship?

5. Discuss the basic idea of transubstantiation. What is the evangelical view of Holy Communion? Is there only one?

Worship during the Medieval Period

1. Describe the "what" and "who" of monasticism.

2. Which distinctive singing style was developed in a monastery; why and by whom was it developed?

3. Name the person who pioneered what later developed into the modern system of musical notation?

4. Which significant event happened in 1054, for what was it known, and how did this event affect the future of the church?

5. Who claims to be the "original" church and why?

Worship and the Reformation

1. Describe what happened on October 31, 1517. List where it happened (city and place), why it happened, and the main players involved. Also, discuss which developments resulted from this critical event in history?

2. List names of those who are widely known as the original Reformers?

3. List three worship practices to which the Reformers desired to return.

4. Describe a typical early Dutch Anabaptist service. Which components are still practiced in Protestant worship services today?

5. Discuss the concept of Free Worship.

Diverse Worship

1. Through which medium did many early Americans learn doctrine?

2. What was developed in high-volume due to the influence of the Reformation?

3. Which region in American inspired many of the early hymns?

4. Name several prominent hymn writers of the era?

5. What began to appear in Protestant worship services by the 16th and 17th centuries, which put an end to 1,000 years of silence?

WORSHIP AND THE AWAKENINGS IN EUROPE AND AMERICA

1. Which Englishman contributed to the Great Awakening in America?

2. Which men were influential in leading many to Christ at several prominent universities in America?

3. Describe the revival in 1801, along with one of its great preachers. Which type of revival meetings began in the wilderness?

4. How did many pioneers express themselves through worship in the frontier?

5. What has happened repeatedly throughout American history that has caused people to turn to God?

Worship and the Great Revivals of the 19th through the 21st Centuries

1. Which revival spilled over from England between 1820 and 1850 that continued to affect many American cities for Christ?

2. Which famous songwriter was the president of the American Sunday School Union in the 1830s, and which song is he well known for writing?

3. Name the great evangelist who started out as a lawyer and his music partner who together influenced many changes to worship in the church. What are some of the changes?

4. The San Francisco Earthquake of 1906 influ-

enced which movement? Describe the emphasis of this revival and the characteristics of worship for which it was established

5. Which Baby Boomer revival spawned CCM? What movement came after that, and what influence does it have on worship today?

Postmodernism and the Future of Worship in the Church

1. What are three chronological periods, along with their dates, that help in understanding how people view God and the world at particular times in history?

2. Describe Postmodernism and list the major philosophical suppositions of this ideology.

3. What makes the Word of God unique in every age of history, and what does it offer to future generations?

4. How does one reach a postmodern culture for Christ, and in what way might worship and music play a role?

5. Describe the worship style to which many Millennials are drawn. Why do you suppose that is true?

Conclusion

1. What does Semper Reformanda mean, and what does it have to do with worship?

2. List several principles that must be employed to guide and safeguard a biblical practice of worship.

3. List the two commandments of Jesus, one found in Matthew 22 and the other in Matthew 28, which are pivotal for understanding worship and

the mission of the church. How do they work together?

4. What is the ultimate purpose of salvation and evangelism?

5. Discuss some observations of the history of worship, reflecting on interesting patterns and human tendencies along the way. In what practical ways can the church propagate biblical worship for future generations?

You have a story.
We want to publish it.

Everyone has as a story to tell. It might be about something you know how to do, or what has happened in your life, or it may be a thrilling, or romantic, or intriguing, or heart-warming, or suspenseful story, starring a cast of characters that have been swimming around in your imagination.

And at Wyatt House Publishing, we can get your story onto the pages of a book just like the one you are holding in your hand. With professional interior design and a custom, professionally designed cover built just for you from the start, you can finally see your dream of being an author become reality. Then, you will see your book listed with retailers all over the world as people are able to buy your book from wherever they are and have it delivered to their home or their e-reader.

So what are you waiting for? This is your time.

visit us at
www.wyattpublishing.com
for details on how to get started becoming a published author right away.

www.ingramcontent.com/pod-product-compliance
Lightning Source LLC
Chambersburg PA
CBHW022123040426
42450CB00006B/813